To my children, Jon and Karrie
M.W.
To my beautiful wife, Gretchen
S.S.

Book Design and Production by
Art & International Productions
Jim Tilly & Sasha Sagan

Copyright © 1996 by Marcia Wakeland
Illustrations copyright ©
by Alexander Sagan

Published by:
Misty Mountain Publishing
P.O. Box 773042
Eagle River, Alaska 99577
1-800-750-8166

First Printing October, 1995
Second Printing May, 1996
Printed in China

Library of Congress
Catalog Card Number
95-94217

ISBN 0-9635083-6-9 Hardcover
ISBN 0-9635083-7-7 Paperback

LOON SONG

Written by Marcia Wakeland, illustrations by Sasha Sagan

Misty Mountain Publishing **Eagle River, Alaska**

The cry slipped into my dream
And roused me from a gentle sleep.
A haunting laugh the cry did seem
Filled with shadows deep.

I opened my eyes, slipped out of bed and tiptoed quietly across the cold floor.

It was three o'clock in the morning, but it wasn't dark. From the window of the cabin, I saw the midnight sun hovering on the horizon. The lake was calm and quiet.

It was too early to wake Grandma........but I couldn't wait. I knew who had made that cry.

I slipped out the door and went down to the shore, curling my knees to my chest. Thin threads of mist swirled up from the lake and mosquitoes buzzed about my ears. But I didn't move at all.

A dragonfly danced along the surface of the water. He flew closer and closer. Then he whispered as he passed, "My dear, why are you here?"

"I'm looking for the loon," I whispered back.

"The loon?" the dragonfly asked, landing on my outstretched hand. " Whatever for? You know his reputation--crazy as a loon. He's crazy as he can be."

"But I do know about the loon," I replied, a little puzzled. "Grandma has told me everything. But she never said the loon was crazy."

The cry came again. Dragonfly and I stopped to hear the eerie notes of the song.

"Listen to that," scoffed the dragonfly. "Tell me that isn't strange."

"That's why you think he's crazy?" I asked.

"That's proof enough for me. He sounds like a loon-atic," said dragonfly, laughing. "But he is strange in other ways."

Before I could answer him, he said, "Look... there's the loon now."

I saw a dark shape gliding and sliding in the water
around the far bend of the island. My heart beat faster.

"He's beautiful," I breathed.

"He's strange," said dragonfly.

"He'szzzzzz looney," a new voice buzzed.

I turned to see a fat bumblebee settle in a nearby flower.

"You think the loon is crazy too?" I asked.

"Certainly," she replied. "He's not like the ducks and geese on this lake. The loon diveszzzzzz down and you never know where he iszzzzzz or where he'll come up. A shady character, I'd say."

As if on cue, the loon disappeared as we watched.

"That's not strange," I said. "He dives to escape trouble or to go fishing. Grandma says he can be underwater for five minutes and dive down 200 feet. It's quite remarkable."

My two new friends rolled their eyes and said, "That couldn't be. He's crazy. As crazy as can be."

"Besideszzzz, you haven't seen his eyeszzzzz, "
said the bee. "The eyeszzz of a madman.

Perhaps the loon was curious about me too because he popped up from the water not far away. I didn't say a word. My eyes danced as I followed the black and white markings on his back and neck. Then I looked into his deep red eyes. And his deep red eyes looked back.

"Scientists think the color of his eyes helps him to see under water when he dives," I whispered to the others.

"A likely explanation," said the dragonfly.
I watched the loon carefully, not wanting to miss a thing.
The loon seemed friendly. I smiled, hoping he would come closer.

"Stay away, madman," hissed dragonfly.

"Watch out, loon-atic" buzzed the bee.
The loon looked startled and disappeared underwater as suddenly as he came.

"You've hurt his feelings," I cried.

"Nonsense, he has no feelings," croaked a voice nearby.

I turned to see a frog lounging on a nearby lily pad.

"You should have more respect," I said. "The loon's ancestors date back over 10 million years to the age of dinosaurs."

"He really is from the Dark Ages," dragonfly replied.

"Maybe that explains why he can't even walk on dry land," bee said, giggling. "He falls over."

I knew they wouldn't listen, but I said, "Loons are born with their legs set far back on their bodies. It's hard for them to balance when they walk."

"My point exactly," said bee.

"Doesn't belong here," said dragonfly.

"And.....look at your friend now," frog said, pointing out to the lake.

I could see the loon
raising up on the water, flapping
and splashing his great dark wings
in a strange, exotic dance.

"He's gone a little off the deep end,
I'd say," smirked the frog.

I sighed. "That is just how the loon preens
himself. It makes him look more handsome."

The frog replied,
"It is obvious that
you refuse to see.
The loon is crazy,
crazy as can be,"

I was sure they were wrong, but how could I prove it? I watched the loon out on the lake, paddling slowly into some grasses on a far shore.

"Have you ever met the loon?" I asked.

"Certainly not," said dragonfly.

"Too risky," said bee.

"Whatever for?" said the frog.

"Well, I'm going to meet him," I said. " I think he wants to be friends."

I set off along the shore. I didn't turn around but I could hear that my new friends weren't far behind.

It wasn't long before I
heard the loon's call close by.
I stopped and peeked through
the bushes.

"Oh, my," I whispered.

"What is it?" asked dragonfly.

"Is it scary?" asked bee.

"Come and see," I said.

I stepped out onto the shore and my
three friends followed close behind.

"He's all dressed up," said dragonfly.
"He'szzz got a girlfriend," buzzed the bee.
"Jumping Jehosophat! He's getting married!"
said the frog.
The loon turned slowly in the water to look at us.
"Let me introduce my bride," said the loon.

We stayed a long time on the shore that early morning, talking and laughing, and celebrating the marriage. The loons tried to teach me how to sing like them. Everyone laughed.

Then the loons called to one another and their song echoed across the lake. It was wild, rich and full of mystery. When the last notes ended, we all sat quietly for a time.

"Grandma will be wondering where I am," I said, yawning.

"And we must let you get off on your honeymoon," said dragonfly.

"Yes, time to leave the two love birdszzzzzz alone," buzzed the bee.

The frog didn't say anything at first. Then he bowed to the loon and said, "Please pardon us for calling you crazy. We were crazy to judge you."

The loons bowed back. Then they glided away into the light of the early dawn.

I wandered back to the cabin and slid into bed,
The notes of loonsong filling my head.
It lulled me back into a dreamy twilight.......
A loonsong, a love song, on a midsummer's night.

Loons will defend the nest ferociously. If you see a loon in a "penguin dance" where he rises up with wings folded, stamping the water, it is a sure signal that the nest or young are close by. Avoid aggravating the loon in this way as the dance is exhausting for the bird and may harm him.

Note from the Author

I grew to love the haunting call of the loon while canoeing the many lakes of Alaska where I make my home. But loons live throughout North America, Europe and Asia. There are different types of adult loon songs, and although experts vary slightly on the classification, most include these different calls: the *tremolo* that sounds like a nervous laugh, the *wail* that sounds like the howl of a wolf, the *yodel* that is used by the male to mark his territory, and the soft *hoot* used to call the mate or chicks. Actually, there is a fifth call, a *mew* that sounds like a baby's cry and is used to reassure chicks, but it is rarely heard by humans.

No one is sure where the phrase "crazy as a loon" came from. It may be the strange call of the loon, but there are also reports of "rogue loons" who may not have chicks of their own and kill the chicks of other loons.

Loons are fascinating and mysterious and I couldn't include all the interesting facts about loons in my story. If you would like to learn more, try taking this quiz about loons.

 # LOON QUIZ

1. How many species of loons are there?

2. Loons mate for life. True or false?

3. How long do loons live?

4. Loons are birds of the Northland and never fly south. True or false?

5. How fast can a loon fly?

6. Why does it take so long for a loon to take off from the water?

7. How could speeding boats harm a loon's nest?

8. How many eggs are in a loon nest?

9. Loons can live close to humans. True or false?

ANSWERS:
1. The Arctic, the Pacific, the red-throated, the yellow-billed, and the common. 2. True and False. It was formerly thought that loons mated for life and some do. But biologists now find evidence that loons maybe more faithful to the same lake than the same mate. 3. 15-30 years. 4. False. Loons winter on the east and west coasts of the U.S. as far south as California and North Carolina. They aren't as noticeable in these climates because they turn a dull gray color and their eyes turn from red to brown. 5. They can fly up 100 miles per hour. 6. Unlike other birds, the loon's bones are solid, not hollow, making their bodies heavier. Also, although they have a long wing span, their wings are relatively narrow for their body size. 7. The wash from the boat could flood the loon nest. 8. Usually one, but occasionally two. They hatch in 27 days. 9. True. Loons can adapt to humans if the water is good, there is abundant food and humans don't interfere with the nests.

Marcia Wakeland grew up in Iowa, but has lived in Alaska for over 20 years. Her favorite retreat is a place called Loon Lake where her family has a log cabin and loons sing their song. Marcia is also the author of *The Big Fish; An Alaskan Fairy Tale.*

Sasha Sagan is an internationally recognized artist and illustrator who currently lives in Anchorage, Alaska. He has designed and illustrated numerous books in Russia and America, including *The Big Fish; An Alaskan Fairy Tale, Puffin, A Journey Home* and *Hal's Magical Cruise - Alaska.*

Special thanks for technical advice from Nancy Tankersley of the Alaska Dept. of Fish and Game and Hans Bernard, loon ornithologist.